There Will Be Silence While You Wait

poems by

Mark Jackley

Plain View Press
P. O. 42255
Austin, TX 78704

plainviewpress.net
sb@plainviewpress.net
512-441-2452

Copyright Mark Jackley 2009. All rights reserved.
ISBN: 978-1-935514-24-4
Library of Congress Number: 2009932100

Cover art: iStock.com
Cover design by Susan Bright

Acknowledgements

Acknowledgment is made to the following publications in which these poems first appeared: "Appalachian Night," in *A Gallery Of Writing*, December 1993; "Immigrant," in *Poesy*, Winter 2004; "Telephone Pole," in *Pebble Lake Review*, Summer 2005; "When Gil Told The Office His Wife Had Terminal Cancer," in *Timber Creek Review*, October 2004; "What's In My Christmas Stocking," in *Barbaric Yawp*, April 2004; "Breaking Up," in *The Clark Street Review*, Spring 2004; "To The Cat I Starved For Days In The Year Of Rage And Lawyers," in *Facets*, August 2006; "Reading Your Love Note, I Get Butterflies," in *Foliate Oak*, May 2005; "A Dog I Saw In The Midst Of An Ugly Divorce," in *Alba*, December 2005; "The Insurance Company Puts Me On Hold," in *Lazy Frog Press*, Spring 2002; "Returning From The Clinic," in *Poetry Depth Quarterly*, July-September 2003; "A Small White House In Winter," "Holiday Shopping," and "Glimpsed While Stuck In Traffic," in 3rd *Muse*, January-March 2006; "When A Truck Smashed Into My Car Like The Fist Of God" and "Middle Age," in *2 River*, Winter 2006; "Gato Barbieri," "As He Has For Eighty Years, He Reads The Morning Paper" in *Hiding Kayak*, April 2008; "Shit Job," in *Word Slaw*, April 2008; "The Morning Sun" and "Western," in *The Grand Rapids Literary Review*, August 2007; "Locks," in *Ducts*, Winter 2007; "Why I Ate The Chocolate Bar," in *Melic Review*, February 2006; "Rain" in *Elegant Thorn Review*, March 2007; "The Motel We Stayed In After You Lost Your Kids In Court," in *Pawpars*, October 2008; "To An Apple," and "Quilt," in *Inertia Magazine*, October 2008; "A Small White House," in *The Honeyland Review*," October 2008; "Obit," "The Moment" and "Rain," in *Best Poem*, January 2009; "One Rainy Christmas, Alone, I Went To 7-11," in *Falling Star Magazine*, Fall 2006; "Hospital Coffee," in *Silent Actor*, 2007; "Elegy," in *Essence*, 2008; "Waiting for An Abortion," in *Ocean Diamond*, Winter 2008; "What My Father Smoked," in *Ballard Street Poetry Journal*, Summer 2007; "Wedding Ring," in *Mississippi Crow*, 2008; "After I Laid Him Off, I Drove Him Home," in *A Little Poetry*, January 2007; "Laughing With a Friend About Our Outlaw Past" and "Afterwards, I Rub Your Back And Begin To Drift," in *The Dublin Quarterly*, September-December, 2007; "Divorce Decree," in *Apt*, 2006; "What The Home Inspector Won't Find," in *Nantahala Review*, Summer-Fall 2007; "Wet, Plush Lawns, 4 A.M.," in *Tonopah Review*, 2008; "Man Eating A Burrito, Waiting For The Movie To Start" and "Round Midnight," in *Baker's Dozen*, 2007; "Wives," in *Munyori Poetry Journal*, November-December 2007; "Lawn Flamingos" and "The Insomniac Wants To Curl Up Somewhere," in *anderbo.com*, Spring 2009; "Recently Divorced," in *Mochila Review*, 2009. Poems in this collection have also appeared in three chapbooks: *Brevities* (Ginninderra Press, 2007); *Into the River Somewhere* (Finishing Line Press, 2007); and *Cracks and Slats* (Amsterdam Press, 2008).

Contents

Appalachian Night	7
A Small White House In Winter	8
Telephone Pole	9
Insomnia, Chatham County	10
When Gil Told the Office His Wife Had Terminal Cancer	11
Proximities	12
Returning From the Clinic	13
Breaking Up	14
To the Cat I Starved For Days In the Year Of Rage and Lawyers	15
Locks	16
A Dog I Saw In the Midst Of an Ugly Divorce	17
What's In My Christmas Stocking	18
When a Truck Smashed Into My Car Like the Fist Of God	19
Immigrant	20
September 11, 2001	21
The Insurance Company Puts Me On Hold	22
The Evening Song Of the Ice Cream Truck	23
Glimpsed While Stuck In Traffic	24
Holiday Shopping	25
Middle Age	26
In a Diner a Middle-Aged Couple Runs Out Of Things To Say	27
After I Laid Him Off, I Drove Him Home	28
The Flowers I Leave At Your Grave	29
An Elderly Woman Staring Into a Boarded-Up Store	30
Fatalities	31
First Night In a Strange New House	32
Laughing With a Friend About Our Outlaw Past	33
What My Father Smoked	34
What You Are	35
Leaning Into Curves	36
To the Hobo Who Flipped Me the Bird When I Waved	37
Why I Ate the Chocolate Bar	38
Afterwards I Rub Your Back and Begin To Drift	39
Rain	40
Little Evening Prayer	41
One Rainy Christmas, Alone, I Went To 7-11	42
'Round Midnight	43
As He Has For Sixty Years, He Reads the Morning Paper	44
Shit Job	45
Western	46
To an Apple	47

At the Hopper Exhibit	48
The Insomniac Wants To Curl Up Somewhere	49
The Morning Sun	50
What the Home Inspector Won't Find	51
Lawn Flamingos	52
Wives	53
Scattering My Dog's Ashes	54
Quilt	55
Napping On a Cloudy Day	56
Drinking Behind the Bowling Alley, Canal Zone '74	57
Cosmology	58
Nineteen, Working Construction	59
Divorce Decree	60
Man Eating a Burrito Before the Movie Starts	61
Gato Barbieri	62
Poet and Daughter	63
Reading Your Love Note, I Get Butterflies	64
Sunset Fires	65
A Small White House	66
The Motel We Stayed In After You Lost Your Kids In Court	67
Wet Plush Lawns, 4 AM	68
Wedding Ring	69
Elegy	70
Waiting For an Abortion	71
Hospital Coffee	72
Truth	73
You Cooked Cheeseburgers At Midnight	74
The Last Time I Saw You Alive	74
The Moment	75
Recently Divorced	76
Rain	77
Afterward	78
About the Author	79

Appalachian Night

Enfolded by pure darkness
a train slips through the hills,
past the occasional litter of homes
leaking yellow light.

In a kitchen window
the silhouette of an enormous man who thinks,
gazing at the train,
he could love anyone on board.

A Small White House In Winter

Its sober wood, unblinking,
is cousin to the coffin.
I have one suggestion
for myself: When the coils
of the stove flare red
and fingertips lift cup to tongue,
and the heat is good,
pretend you hold a star.

Telephone Pole

Bolted to a cross,
cables slump,
fraught with talk,
clumsy, loving
stabs at something.
Quietly, it grows dark.

If resurrection comes,
perhaps we will be birds
perched on the wires,
without reason
rising into silence.

Insomnia, Chatham County

Witnessing, not disappearing.
Soft rain on the trailer.
Slow blue light,
each quiet, unrepeatable breath
in these dark woods.

When Gil Told the Office His Wife Had Terminal Cancer

No one, least of all me,
wept or wailed.
No one pounded his fists
against the walls
or chanted in prayer.
For we are not a primitive people,
so we stared, mumbled regrets
and let the shadow pass,
then slipped back into
the coolness of our cubes.

Proximities

No one knew where his father was.
I was on the toilet, naked.
His mother, whom I barely knew,
was naked on her vast white bed.

When he, eight years old,
cried out for a moment in the darkness
of his room, dreaming, racing,
he too was far away.

Returning From the Clinic

You said you wanted comfort food
and so we stopped along the way
for chicken and dumplings,
mashed potatoes and gravy, a slice of pie.

That is, after taking a life,
we nourished ourselves, or tried.
We ate in silence, broken
by the scrape of knives.

Breaking Up

We picked up lethal shards of glass
from the carpets and the stairs.
Put twisted picture frames
and ripped-up photos into piles.
Yanked my daughter's bicycle
out from under barbells,
swept up shattered dishes,
vacuumed cat shit in the hall.
Wiped the now bare walls.
Stared at busted lamps
and splintered chairs.
The entire time, we uttered not a sound.
Then we tossed it all into big black bags
and left it on the curb,
where under the morning stars
it disappeared for good.

To the Cat I Starved For Days
In the Year Of Rage and Lawyers

Guilty of wanting
love, food,
you will always be
on the kitchen floor
tearing the wrapping from
a loaf of bread,
fangs bared,
something I will never
forget, my fierce companion,
who are gnawing still.

Locks

All those times I changed the locks
after we fought like vipers.
All those hundreds of dollars
spent to keep you out.
All those glittering keys,
their little teeth bared
and yet I address you still,
proof there is no door.

A Dog I Saw In the Midst Of an Ugly Divorce

He stood like a pirate
in the middle of the road,
howling, grinning. Four a.m.
Everyone else in bed,
except for I, who also wore
the darkness like a cape
and chased what sped at me,
the gathering wildness of the day.

What's In My Christmas Stocking

Forty-four winters.
A bottle of gin.
Two ex-wives.
A dead ex-girlfriend.
One sweet daughter.
Two abortions.
A custody war.
A restraining order.
Some useless poems,
and at bottom
the urge to cry
like a man never does.

When a Truck Smashed Into My Car Like the Fist Of God

God knows why
I wasn't hurt,
but I was blown out
of my shoes, so
I hobbled home
in my stocking feet
like a holy fool
who wanders the Moroccan sands
or Tibetan slopes,
feeling every pebble,
each step on the earth.

Immigrant

For AJW

The last time in Oncology
you gave me a look I'd never seen,
one that drifted like the shadows
on the cold machines,
poor as your dressing gown,
sad as your thin bones,
an immigrant squinting at a photo
of the brother left at home.

September 11, 2001

Returning in darkness
to her mother's, my two-year-old glanced
at our neighborhood woods
and whispered, *Listen, monsters.*

Before I could reason with her
she climbed into my arms,
placed a tiny hand on my mouth
and commanded, *Shhh.*

The Insurance Company Puts Me On Hold

Finally, truth, and from the unlikeliest lips.
Godlike, it only exists

in my head it seems, a voice on tape:
There will be silence while you wait.

The Evening Song Of the Ice Cream Truck

is a call to prayer,
to savor what is
cool and sweet
in the melting night.

Glimpsed While Stuck In Traffic

Suddenly, wings.
A flock of geese
hovers in plush air
and touches down,
as if from Bering twilight
onto tundra, proving
that even by the dumpster
of the Taco Loco,
inches above the asphalt and the oil,
there is sky.

Holiday Shopping

Winter light, the day's last,
on the bricks of bulging stores.
The light of Vermeer,
the light of Robert Frank,
Einstein's light.
The golden light of every silver breath.
Your light and mine,
the gift we briefly own,
the one we can't exchange.

Middle Age

This line of my face is a river.
A villager stoops, hauls water.
His shoulders burn. If he's lucky,
he will carry it a long way.

In a Diner a Middle-Aged Couple Runs Out Of Things To Say

white table like a glacier
dividing China and Tibet,

a place where things disappear as quietly
as the snow leopard, whose

dark eyes and twitching tail,
same heat that made the stars,

are a memory cold
as coffee in still hands

After I Laid Him Off, I Drove Him Home

His molten anger soon
sputtering into sadness,
hardening into fear
of telling his wife,
and the coolness
of his darkening kitchen,
my white hands on the table,
my tongue curled, still
as anything in Pompeii.

The Flowers I Leave At Your Grave

Not wanting the wind and rain to scatter them
yet forgetting a pot,
I dig a hole, using
my ice-scraper, planting
the stems as best as I can.
Done, I stare at your name
in wonder, clutching the muddy tool
bought to help me see.

An Elderly Woman Staring Into a Boarded-Up Store

Cunning as a river,
inscrutable as a glacier,
firm as a wave,
the sun, artisan
of light and shadow, carves
the geography of the moment,
strangest place of all,
not found on any map.

Fatalities

They pulled the sheet over the body.
A neighbor strode right past

to check his mail. I did the same
when I got home, my fingers,

no prayer to hold, no Heaven
to receive it, coolly

leafed the pages of
a magazine, my rosary.

First Night In a Strange New House

Just divorced,
I follow my heart,
blind men bumping in the dark.

Laughing With a Friend About Our Outlaw Past

But the tale of Dave Revard
and his not-quite moustache,
his feathered hair
and corduroy jacket,
the cops in Mississippi
who shot him dead,
the marijuana
exploits, the tequila
and the skid marks is,
judging from the hushing
of our tone, almost
a trigger all its own
for two men with divorces,
child support and parents
who will soon stop breathing.
We won't see it coming.
Quietly, we slide
the gun back into the drawer.

What My Father Smoked

Borkum Riff, tamped into his pipe,
his finger spade-like,
tobacco moist as earth
to which the men he lost
in war returned,
whom I doubt he ever buried
in his armchair in the dark.

A sudden flame – I see him glow,
wreathed in smoke, palming ashes.

What You Are

For Mary, in memory

Maybe you are luminous.
I doubt you are particular,
a cup of snow, the stillness
of a leaning rake,
cars abandoned deep
in grasses quiet as the sea,
shy gray rain that tiptoes
when the moon winks.
You are not my stumbling
tongue, my cranium's
cartoons. I get it, dear.
Simply, you are not.

Leaning Into Curves

the light is on the door
unlocks her hips and palms
are warm the moon
and stars are lifting
and the engine
cools in the wet
summer night

To the Hobo Who Flipped Me the Bird When I Waved

You are not Walt Whitman,
forget your long white beard and mane,
the way you loafed
on the Oklahoma grass, springing up
electrically to say that I,
in my glittering car,
could go fuck myself.

On second thought, you are.

Why I Ate the Chocolate Bar

Because Oprah told me not to.
Because you couldn't stop me.
Not because Eve ate the apple. I'll invent my own sins, thanks.
Because I didn't get laid last night. Thanks for nothing, Eve.
Because my mouth was empty save for dry, tasteless words.
Because at twenty I was drunk on life and thumbed from D.C. to L.A.
Because my life is half over.
Because I don't ride a Harley.
Because I'm chained to a desk all day.
Because we used to roam forests.
Because chocolate bars in the grave will taste like dirt and worms.

Afterwards I Rub Your Back and Begin To Drift

My fingers are old men
hobbling in a garden,
who blink and step with care
over the uneven
land they know by heart,
yet it still surprises
when a little tilling
produces miracles.

Rain

It bumps against the window,
staggered and ecstatic
to bring the news: The heavens
cup the earth, and now
the world is small, and quiet,
as a breath. The cat
blinks and wonders. Tell me,
friend, the rain is not
a gift but a cold fact,
and I will take your word
in my hand and skip it
over my wet heart.

Little Evening Prayer

May I lose
possession
of my self,
every scrap
that I have
bought and sold
and be the
shopping
cart alone,
shining
in the apocalyptic
parking lot,
seagulls drifting,
lost or not,
in pink
and orange
liquid dusk
that lifts into
the river
somewhere.

One Rainy Christmas, Alone, I Went To 7-11

Not to overstate it, but I had a lovely time.
The only thing I wanted, a cup of coffee, was actually good.
The manager, from Bangladesh, smiled and said nothing
as I scanned a Rolling Stone, without buying it.
I watched people trickle in and make their small purchases,
a paper, beer, fake firewood, cheap wine, a bar of soap.
We were happy – well, I was happy – in this modest place,
a picture of Zen efficiency, where it was warm and dry,
beyond whose little brightness the remains of the year
gurgled down the gutters, freely, without complaint.

'Round Midnight

The whoosh of the air conditioner
brings to mind Ben Webster's
horn as Billie moans. I adore my wife, thank God
she is asleep at last.
I curl up with a book. My father,
thirty years ago, pours his last martini,
clutches "The Lonely Silver Rain"
by John D. McDonald.
In a quiet corner
of Des Moines my father's father
closes his eyes to the Great Depression,
blows on his trombone,
for even white men get the blues,
it is something that we love.

As He Has For Sixty Years, He Reads the Morning Paper

Then,
in silence and gray light,
he works the smudged ink
from his fingers, trying,
a ritual of faith
and survival, to
wash his hands, cold
water and deep sink,
of the crumpled world.

Shit Job

Night comes and I stare
at the spruce in my front yard.
It teeters in the breeze
like a shy dancer
holding the hem of her dress,
on the verge of leaping,
any second now,
towards dark applause.

Western

Her soon-to-be ex-husband,
who worked for the C.I.A.,
a bit of a cowboy, owned a gun,
she whispered. We crouched down
behind the door of his soon-to-be
ex-home as he pounded with his fists,
hollering ultimatums.
It was like the O.K. Corral,
though unlike Wyatt Earp
I trembled as I slowly
turned the knob. Not knowing
I existed, he
dropped his scowl and blinked,
and didn't say a word,
unsure what to make of
this latest change of script.

To an Apple

You seem to know there is
no frost until there is,
little Buddha, master
of the art of being
in the moment though
you ripen in the sun,
rendered brilliantly
by God or Paul Cezanne.

At the Hopper Exhibit

For Bob Blair

The mythical horse on the Mobil sign
soars along the treetops,
sailing to the place everyone gazes towards,
where the woman in the hotel room
is not alone, forsaken,
the movie usher isn't bored
staring at her shoes,
where the lady in her summer dress
somehow finds a bliss
greater than standing in the light
in her summer dress,
where the moment is enough,
chop suey slowly savored,
far beyond the frame,
where horses have wings.

The Insomniac Wants To Curl Up Somewhere

Like a cinnamon roll curling
into its soft, sweet center.
Like the cat curling
into herself, finding
warmth, peace, knowing
there is nothing to do
but love oneself. This
is where the problem starts.

The Morning Sun

The blue flannel shirt you wore
when we made love in your trailer
was nearly as worn as my memories
of making love in your trailer.

I can taste the coffee
I sipped when I awoke
and sat at your kitchen counter
naked, and the honey

from my toast is stuck,
a little bit, anyway,
in a corner of my lips,
and you lick it off.

I remember you kept your Christmas lights
up all year and that
there were many cracks and slats
the morning sun shone through.

What the Home Inspector Won't Find

First, the ghost of the seller's wife,
who recently died. Burns.
Second, the sadness festering,
mold after rain. Third, and most vexing,
the flaw in the master plan
of this habitation wired for,
crackling with pain.

Lawn Flamingos

October. Topped with frost,
they migrate not much less
than commuters and bus drivers
flecked with gray who pass them
every morning, dreaming
of pink summers,
checking for lost plumage
in the rear-view.

Wives

It has taken me only three
to figure it out.
Each morning,
the cat cries and cries
at the basement door.
I open it and she
stands there, not moving
or saying help me but
hello hello hello.

Scattering My Dog's Ashes

They were not feathery like the soul
but hard like her head,
stuffed into a Tupperware-like
container, which was sealed

more tightly than Fort Knox.
I loved that she obeyed
not one order that I gave,
as on that hillside when

I tearfully muttered, "Goddamn it,
come out" and fifteen minutes
later I was still
prying off the lid.

Quilt

For my daughter

A few minutes of cartoons
as we spoon soup,
January dusk,
perhaps are quilted like

patchwork into something
I will reach for in
my last winter,
when I am never warm.

In that bare flat,
reruns on TV,
hands that cradled you
will finger every seam.

Napping On a Cloudy Day

though the rain
comes on small
feet we are going far

Drinking Behind the Bowling Alley, Canal Zone '74

It skitters like an armadillo when I am stuck in traffic
or fingering divorce
paperwork, the feeling

that I am still fifteen,
waiting for the Cuna
Indian who ran the place to fill my fishing bucket

with Schlitz, and praying for
facial hair and sex.
The PFC next to me is chafing in strange clothes.

Soon, warm rain. We are hunched in folding chairs,
nearly fetal, hoping
to finish being born.

Cosmology

For Kim

After making love I dream
we are clementines,
sweet and perfect lumps
nestled in our crate
of wood and nails, the plastic
netting is the end
of the world, exactly
where it ought to be.

Nineteen, Working Construction

I'd done nothing but
get up at dawn, slurp
coffee, wolf a biscuit, grip a hammer,
smash walls,
grunt and scratch my balls,
talk dirty with the painters,
smoke and spit and know
I could die happy.

Divorce Decree

After all the jawing,
all the heated words,
it came quietly
in the iron stillness
of the mailbox whose
mouth was hanging open
in the April breeze,
much like mine.

Man Eating a Burrito
Before the Movie Starts

He bows his head in the church-like stillness,
tenderly regarding
the miracle of chicken, rice and beans.

When a God-like voice booms
from the screen, he,
slowly licking his fingers,
rebel without a napkin,
commits the heresy
of being filled already

with happiness.
He burps,
ignores the coming attractions.

Gato Barbieri

Last Tango scarf,
wrap-around shades
for near-blindness. Stoic
ferocity of a jungle chieftain.
Sam Spade fedora.
And the horn, a piece
of exposed plumbing,
all that matters, the gleaming
guts of the man.

Poet and Daughter

I am my words,
ink and pixels,

you my link
to eternity,

the bright and vast
intensity

of the
empty page.

Reading Your Love Note, I Get Butterflies

Some are Monarchs
who have come a long way,
drawn by the warm wings of your voice.
Before they grew wings they crept,
caterpillars of doubt.

Others are brilliant Blue Morphos
from the Panamanian jungles.
The males have brighter colors
because they are more desperate.

All make barely audible clicks
to say things to each other,
softer even than
my keyboard typing this.

Sunset Fires

On a Friday evening when
we are old and not too horny,
sitting on the steps,
wiggling toes in the dirt,
and the oak trees and the maples
beg the sun, their lover,
not to flee as they embrace
stars and birds and other
forms of lust in their rough arms,
let us, dear, applaud
as loudly as we can
with soft smiles.

A Small White House

May I, when I walk
out the door for good
know the peace of cool
walls and concrete basement
floor, of empty rooms
silent as a corner
spider weaving something
fine and silver, pulsing
in the slightest breeze,
a breath that comes and goes
through these darkened halls,
God knows why.

The Motel We Stayed In After You Lost Your Kids In Court

August heat and stillness,
black chant of crickets.
Worn wooden floors,
torn screen door —
like an abandoned cabin
into which a wounded
animal crawled to nose
its own blood and wail.

Wet Plush Lawns, 4 AM

Good night, married woman whose house I slink away from.
Good night, traveling husband, and regrets.
Good night, teenage daughter
who choked to death from asthma
in this very home. Good night, barroom tears.
Good night, binge drinking,
drunken fucking, too.
Good night, forgetfulness, filthy and delicious.
Good night, black silence, once again I see
it is right for you alone
to have the last word.

Wedding Ring

I imagine it being eyeballed
by a carp slowly
trolling the bottom of
the Rappahannock River,
blinking in the cold
depths, disbelieving
a lure that for some reason
no longer shines.

Elegy

Your voice was an ember glowing
in the small darkness
of the telephone.
Information, please —
I hear you still, the darkness
is immense now, who
strung the lines and how
does the damn thing work?

Waiting For an Abortion

I remember there was a coat rack
in the waiting room
with gleaming brass hooks,
apropos of nothing.
Babies are not speared
but vacuumed, sucked away.
But I can see it still.
It is the dead of summer,
the rack is empty save
for my conscience, limp,
which has a little tag:
Men's medium.

Hospital Coffee

It is weak.
So are bones.
Bitter,
like the truth
of the body
breaking.
Black,
like the fear
of falling
asleep
and waking
into the slow
drip
of the doctor's
words,
which easily
could burn.

Truth

The heart bumps along like a bus.
Sooner or later you notice
a rider who stares. Hands on her lap,
she chews her lip,
fidgets with buttons.

Dusk. A little rain falls.
Maybe she, like most
on board the 6:05,
won't utter a single word.

You Cooked Cheeseburgers At Midnight The Last Time I Saw You Alive

and for once
I slept

so lover,
peace

will always taste like
melted cheese

salt
fat
grease

The Moment

The paper,
the hands that fold it,
the airplane that takes shape

and flight, the arc, the swoop
and whoosh
the disappearance.

Recently Divorced

They danced, the barfly trying to coax
rhythm from a corpse.
When the music stopped,
she lowered him into a booth,
gently patted him on the back as if tamping dirt
strewn with sharp rocks
over cut roots.

Rain

Heaven-sent to perform mouth-to-mouth on flowers, trees,
it belongs to the scientist, the shaman and persimmons.

It careens down windows like a novice skier,
a spooked colt,
like Liana, ten,
running into the years.

Afterward

The hum of cars approaching climbs
our warm, wet skin.

Otherwise, and blissfully,
no future.

About the Author

Mark Jackley is the author of three chapbooks: *Brevities* (Ginninderra Press), *Into the River Somewhere* (Finishing Line Press) and *Cracks and Slats* (Amsterdam Press). This is his first full-length collection. He lives in Sterling, VA, with his wife, daughter and assorted pets.

www.ingramcontent.com/pod-product-compliance
Lightning Source LLC
Chambersburg PA
CBHW052114070526
44584CB00017B/2476